ROCK KEYBOARD

THE COMPLETE GUIDE WITH AUDIO!

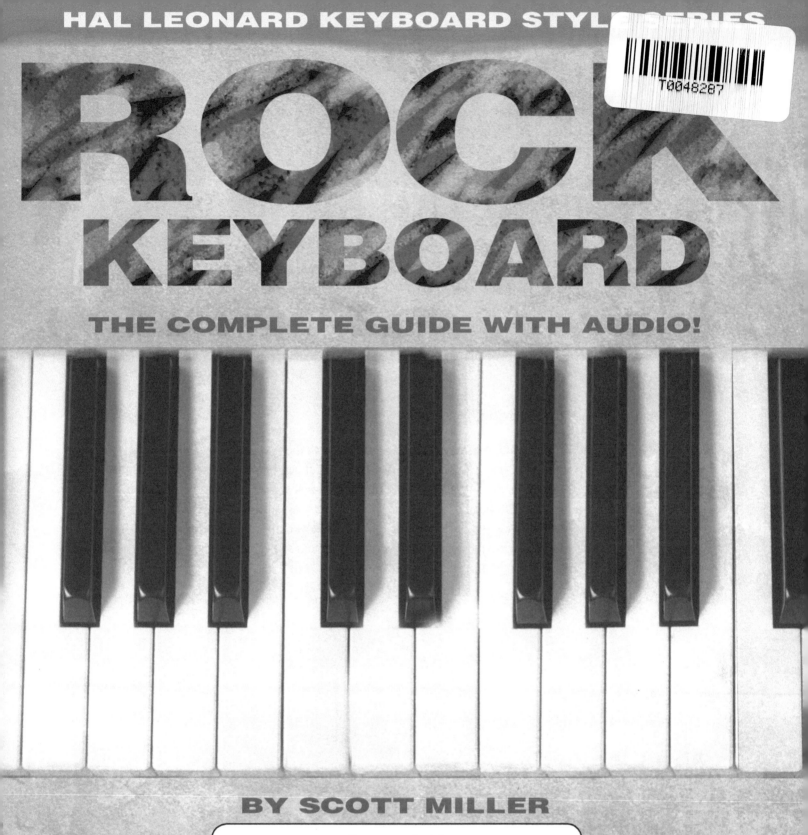

BY SCOTT MILLER

To access audio visit:
www.halleonard.com/mylibrary

7235-4887-1506-9536

ISBN 978-0-634-03981-2

HAL•LEONARD®
CORPORATION
7777 W. BLUEMOUND RD. P.O. BOX 13819 MILWAUKEE, WI 53213

Visit Hal Leonard Online at www.halleonard.com

INTRODUCTION

Welcome to *Rock Keyboard*. If you've ever wanted to play keyboard in a rock band, but weren't sure what to play or how, then you've come to the right place. Whatever your playing level—beginning, intermediate, or advanced—you'll find something here that meets your needs.

In rock, as in many styles of music, a keyboardist is usually either *comping* (e.g., playing chords or other accompaniment behind a vocalist) or *soloing* (playing licks, riffs, fills, etc.). This book gives you ideas for both.

Comping: Each chapter in this book covers a different style of rock. In the first section of every chapter, we'll focus on harmony, chord voicings, bass lines, and other aspects of comping in that style. This is the stuff you need to know in a band situation. What does your right hand play? How about your left hand? What about the rhythms? As a keyboardist, you parts need to sound great on their own but also fit into the groove with the rest of the band.

Soloing: When you're not comping, you're probably soloing—that is, playing a lick or riff that "fills in" or creates a recognizable "hook" in the song. You might also be improvising over a song section. In the "soloing" section of each chapter, we'll cover ideas for creating your own licks and riffs and for improvising with scales and chords.

Rock Keyboards is chock full of authentic rock keyboard parts. Learn them all, and you'll be well on your way to playing your first (or next) gig. Most parts are two-handed but can be played one-handed (treble clef only) if a player prefers. (The bass parts typically double what a bassist would play.) However, it's highly recommended that you practice both hands: this prepares you for playing solo or in a group without a bassist, and improves both your understanding of the music and your coordination as a keyboardist. Also, once you're somewhat comfortable playing these tracks, try tranposing them to different keys. Most progressions and licks can be used in many different scenarios.

Rock on!

—Scott Miller

About the Audio

Each example in this book is included with the accompanying audio tracks. Just listen for the count-off, then join in. The audio features a full band—keyboard, guitar, bass, and drums—so you can hear how your parts fit in with the total groove.

Guitar: Paul Mayasich
Bass: John Iden
Drums: Mark O'Day
Keyboards: Scott Miller

CONTENTS

Chapter 1

CLASSIC ROCK

À la the Rolling Stones, the Doors, Van Morrison, Creedence Clearwater Revival, the Steve Miller Band, Warren Zevon, Fleetwood Mac, and more...

Classic rock artists like the ones above created many legendary songs that still have a timeless sound quality to them. Much of it was the songwriting, but the rest can be attributed to the greatness and simplicity of the parts that each player created on his or her own instrument.

Comping

Four-Bar Vamp (with Turnaround)

A *vamp* is a section of music that can be repeated indefinitely, making it an excellent accompaniment for a vocalist or soloist. Here's a classic Warren Zevon/Rolling Stones type of vamp based on I and V chords in the key of G. The voicings are dominant sevenths (G7 and D7), à la the blues, using simple three-note inversions in the right hand. The *turnaround* at the end (the D7 chord) effectively leads back (or "turns around") back to the beginning.

Notice the bass part: it covers the roots of each chord, with chromatic approaches. Rhythmically speaking, it uses a common "anticipated" feel—the eighth note on the "and" of beat 2 is actually an anticipation of beat 3—which gives the part a rhythmic "kick."

TRACK 1

Two-Bar Vamps

Vamps can be of any length, of course. Here's a great two-bar vamp, repeated to form an eight-bar phrase with a *fill* at the end. The progression is a little more complex, moving from I (C) to I7 (C7) to IV (F) to a V chord substitute (F/G). The voicings are a mix of three- and four-note. The bass supports the chord movement but also creates its own melodic line by mixing roots with other chord tones. The rhythm is once again predominantly eighth notes, with the bass making use of anticipation (on the F/G chord). The fill is a hybrid of blues and pentatonic ideas—using the ♭3rd (E♭), ♭5th (G♭), and the 6th(A). Check out the descending sixth intervals!

You might think this next vamp is in the key of C—the chords C, F, and G would be the I, IV, and V in that key. But the tonic here is G, making this a I–♭VII–IV vamp in the key of G major (or G Mixolydian, if you like—but more on that later). This is another classic and essential rock progression. The extra twist here is that each chord also moves briefly to its own IV chord—e.g., G–C, F–B♭, C–F—a popular ornamental device of classic rock. (To simplify the part, you could take this motion out; it still works.)

The bass plays octaves supporting the root movement; notice the anticipation in bar 2 as well as the chromatic walk-up.

TRACK 3

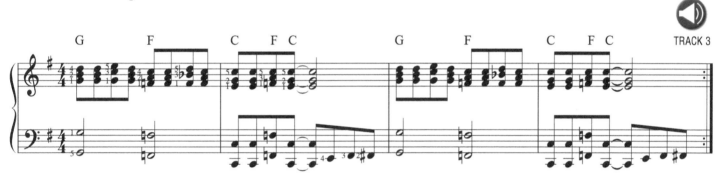

One-Bar Vamp

This next idea is really just a one-bar vamp on a C9 chord, in full five-note voicing. The rhythmically off-kilter bass adds some nice touches: a bluesy ♭3rd-to-3rd motion, and the anticipation of beat 1.

TRACK 4

play 5 times

Minor with Descending Bass

Here's a classic minor idea that involves moving down by half step from the root of the tonic: In G minor, the first two bars move to the IV chord (C) via the chromatic descending bass line (G–F♯–F–E). The next two move back to the tonic via whole-step motion in the bass: E♭–F–Gm.

Notice the four-note voicings in the opening measure, played in "rocking" motion.

TRACK 5

Blues-Based Minor

These next few ideas are all in minor and are all blues-based, borrowing from traditional blues forms, phrasings, and scales.

Two-note voicings can be used to leave more space in the sound, giving the other instruments plenty of room to maneuver. This example in C minor uses fourths and thirds from the C minor/C blues scale to fashion a distinctive riff; notice how it doesn't interfere with the guitar voicings. The progression—four bars on the i chord, two bars on a iv chord, and two bars on the i chord—is basically the first eight bars of a 12-bar blues form.

TRACK 6

Here's another bluesy minor piece: this one is in G minor and goes through a full 12-bar form. The accompaniment here is more obviously chord-based—using thirds to create a distinctive sound in and around the i, iv, and V chords. Watch out for the "stop" after the C7 chord!

TRACK 7

Here's another eight-bar blues-based idea in Cm. This time, the bass line drives the piece with a solid blues riff. (Check out the ♭5th!) The right hand adds chord accents on beat 2, using economical three-note voicings (inversions without the root) for minor sevenths.

TRACK 8

3/4 Time

Looking for something different? This two-chord vamp in 3/4 time should fill the bill. The two-note bass pedal (root and ♭7th) gives it a propulsive but uncertain feel, while the right hand moves back and forth between Cm7 and F chords.

Incidentally, notice the key signature: it's B♭ major. That could make this a ii7–V progression in the key of B♭. Alternatively, you could see it as a i7-IV progression in C minor (but technically, the raised 6th degree, A, would make it C Dorian—a very common mode in rock).

TRACK 9

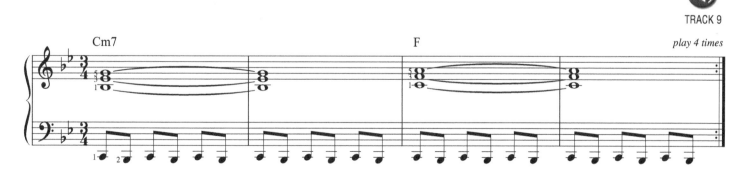

Walking Bass

These next two tracks are both based on the same walking bass line. A *walking bass line* moves in quarter notes (the consistent rhythm feels like "walking"), outlining important chord tones while also maintaining a melodic contour using select non-chord tones and chromatic notes.

Both examples are i9–V7 vamps in C minor. The first uses whole notes—many times, this is all you need to leave the right amount of space for guitar, bass, and drums. The second has an "anticipated" rhythm. Incidentally, both have an underlying "swing" feel.

TRACK 10

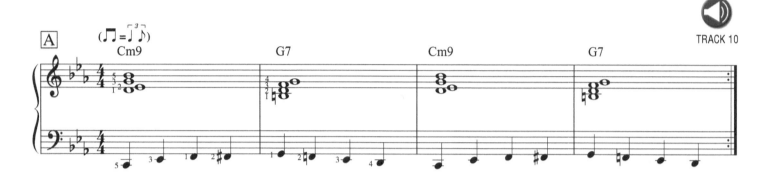

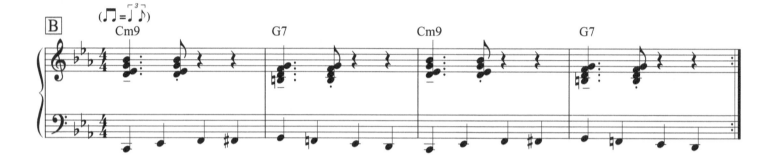

Blues-Based Major (Two-Handed Chords)

Here's a simple eight-bar idea in G major—again, obviously blues-based. Check out the two-handed seventh chord voicings, the chromatic walk-ups, and the distinctive rhythm.

TRACK 11

The One-Bar Dorian Vamp

Here's a classic "pseudo-jazz" vamp that artists like Van Morrison and the Doors were quite fond of. First, look at the key signature: it's G major. Next, notice that the bass is playing fifths outlining Am and Bm. The tonal center is really Am. That makes this a minor vamp built on the second degree of a major scale; in other words, an A Dorian vamp (think of it as A minor with a major 6th degree, F#).

Get comfortable with the bass line first, it's the foundation of the groove. Then add the "anticipated" chords, and play them with a light touch. The right hand fills out the harmony with three-note voicings of minor sevenths, then the idea is extended by moving the whole thing down to D minor (Dm7 to Em7).

TRACK 12

Another Dorian Idea

Here's another vaguely Dorian idea. This time, the bass plays octave roots in quarter notes while the right hand vamps from Am to D to Am7 and then back down. The result is a melodic "hook" over an A pedal. The whole idea is transposed, with some modification, to F, and then the last two bars make a turnaround ending on a V7 chord (E7).

TRACK 13

Soloing

Soloing in the classic rock genre can sound harder than it really is. Good rhythmic phrasing is essential: Practice use of rests (to create space), accents (to create contour), and different note values (to add variety). The solo ideas in this chapter are predominantly blues-based but will work in a variety of contexts.

Minor Pentatonic

The minor pentatonic (1–♭3–4–5–♭7) is an essential scale for soloing over major or minor progressions. It even works for the "pseudo-jazz" Dorian idea we learned earlier.

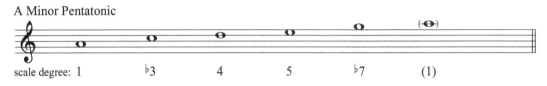

Here's a line based on A minor pentatonic. Try it out by itself, then try it with bass notes in the left hand or with chords. (See the Scales section at the end of this book for minor pentatonic scales in other keys.)

TRACK 14

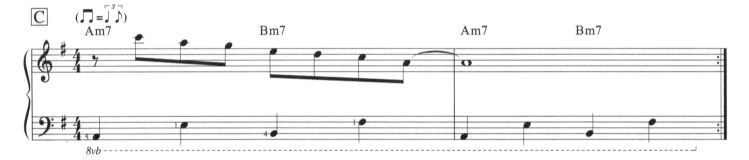

Dyads/Chords

Now try the same line, but start expanding on it. This version riffs off an Am chord, using thirds (dyads). Notice also the space left at the end of the phrase.

TRACK 15

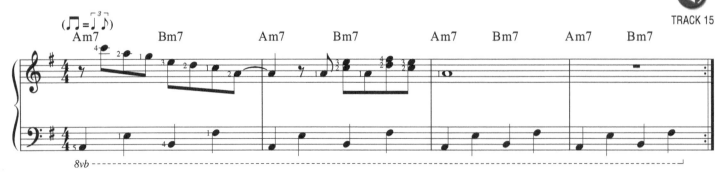

10

Grace Notes

Grace notes are an important part of keyboard soloing: they "bend" a note to give it more life. Pay attention to the direction the grace note is coming from and to where it is going. This phrase adds the ♭5th (E♭) to our A minor pentatonic ideas, giving them a bluesy sound.

TRACK 16

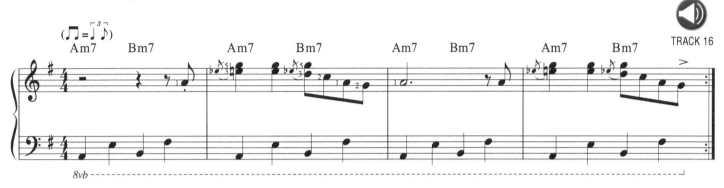

The Blues Scale

Add one note to the minor pentatonic scale, and you get a blues scale: 1–♭3–4–♭5–5–♭7.

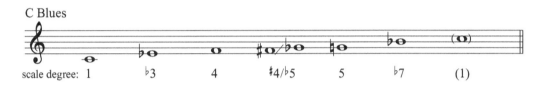

Here's a line based on the C blues scale. Try it out by itself, then try it against a walking bass line like the one shown. Notice the triplets in the right hand; they add variety to the line. Be sure to play with a swing feel throughout.

TRACK 17

Repetition & Variation

A staple of blues-based music is repetition and variation—i.e., a phrase is played once, then repeated, then varied, then possibly repeated again. Here's another C blues idea. Watch how the repetition and variation play out over this eight-bar progression.

TRACK 18

Chapter 2
POP ROCK

À la Billy Joel, Elton John, Supertramp, The Police, Phil Collins, Styx, Queen, Journey, and more...

Unlike classic rock, which borrows frequently from the blues, pop rock tends to favor either diatonic progressions (for ballads) or modal vamps (for upbeat rockers). The triad is a perfect-sized chord in a pop rock band setting. There are many other instruments in a band, and you want to have your own chord voicing whenever possible. Sometimes, a simple triad (three-note chord) is all you need to sound great.

Comping

Octave Bass

On upbeat tunes, an octave part in the left hand typically doubles the bass guitar—creating a propulsive rhythm while firmly establishing the tonality. Styx, Journey, and Billy Joel use this type of "bass doubling" often.

In this vamp, the right hand plays simple triads on top of an eighth-note octave bass. The key is G, and the basic progression is I–♭VII–IV (G-F-C). The F/C chord acts as a IV chord embellishment of the C.

TRACK 19

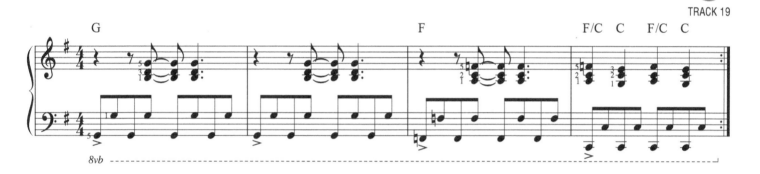

Pedal Point

Here's a similar idea, but the bass stays on G throughout. This creates what's called a *pedal point:* the bass remains fixed on a single note while chords change above it.

Notice the cadence at the end: E♭-F-G. This is a ♭VI–♭VII–I progression, borrowed from parallel minor (G minor). E♭ and F sound good against this octave G pedal because there are no sharp dissonances: In an E♭ chord, G is a 3rd; in an F chord, G is an added 2nd.

TRACK 20

Added 2nds

Here's another triad-based part, but this time, the voicings are four-note, and they're arpeggiated. To add some melodic "bite," a 2nd is also added to each chord. Once again, the left hand plays an octave bass. Notice the progression here: It's a I–IV–V–I in the key of C.

TRACK 21

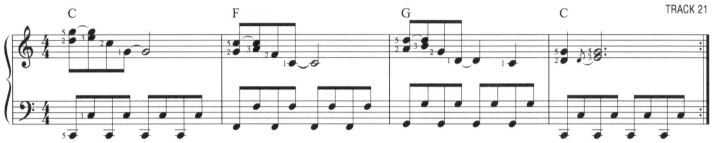

Ballad Accompaniments

Speaking of four-note voicings, this next example is a slow ballad-type progression using triads played in a "rocking" thumb-and-fingers motion. You might hear Elton John, Queen, The Beatles, or other artists use this type of part. Notice the use of passing chords and inversions to create a smooth bass melody.

TRACK 22

This piece is similar in its voicings, but the progression gets a little more harmonically aventurous, featuring a seventh chord (C7) and a V chord substitute (Fm). Notice the descending melody created by the top note of each chord. Also check out the fill in measure 5.

TRACK 23

Here's one more ballad idea, this one using triad voicings in the right hand to occasionally imply other extended chords (like Cm7 and E♭11). The key is A♭ major, and the basic progression is I–iii–IV–V. This accompaniment sounds good on piano or with a digital EP tone or tine patch on your keyboard.

TRACK 24

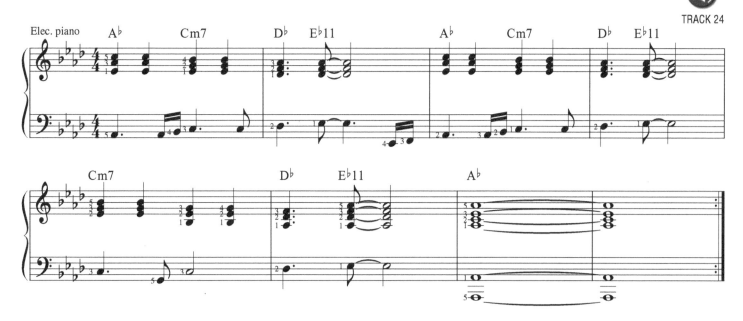

More Advanced Textures

Experimenting with different eighth and sixteenth-note rhythms can add a new dimension to your accompaniments. The following ideas explore rhythmic possibilities for the right and left hands. In the keys of D major and D minor, they employ simple descending basses in the left hand with a mixture of melodic and chord-based ideas in the right.

TRACK 25

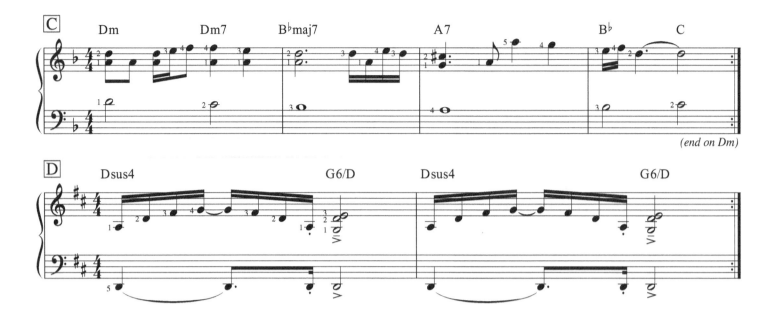

(end on Dm)

Soloing

Often, the keyboard solo line in pop rock is a pre-written melodic phrase rather than a free, improvised solo. This can serve as the "hook" of the song and can be just as effective as an improvised "jam."

The Multi-Purpose Lick

Here's a pre-written idea in C major. It's basically two licks fused together, with no definite harmonic implications. This is a good one because it's not really a scale, nor is it an arpeggio. (Well, it would be a C triad arpeggio, but the F throws that off.)

Lines like these are great to have under your fingers when trying to come up with your own fills or solos. First try it alone, then try adding a simple descending bass line (over a C pedal) as shown. Then try speeding it up a bit, and adding some improvisation.

TRACK 26

Octaves

Here's another pre-written lick, this time using octaves. Again, this line is obviously based on a C tonality, but there are plenty of non-harmonic tones so that it can be harmonized in a variety of ways.

TRACK 27

Four-Note Arpeggios

Arpeggios are always a great soloing source. Here's a I–IV–vi–♭VII progression using four-note voicings of simple triads. The bass is quite simple, too: just octave root notes. Notice the lick over the last chord—it punctuates the end of the four-bar phrase nicely.

TRACK 28

More Non-Chord Tones

Adding a non-chord interval like a second to a simple triad arpeggio is one way of creating an instant soloing idea. Try it out here on V and IV chords (G and F) in the key of C.

TRACK 29

"Modal" Arpeggios

Here's a sort of extension on the previous idea. The right hand plays an arpeggio-type lick, but not of any particular chord. The intervals are a second and a fifth—a juxtaposition that you can move about and harmonize various ways. (I sometimes call these "modal arpeggios"; you're not arpeggiating a chord, per se—more like a chunk of a mode!) The extra twist is the rhythm: a 3+3+2 pattern.

TRACK 30

Chapter 3
BLUES ROCK

À la Eric Clapton, Bonnie Raitt, The Rolling Stones, Robert Cray, Johnny Lang, Blues Traveler, Deep Purple, B.B. King, Buddy Guy, and more...

Blues rock takes the style and structure of blues as its inspiration. Improvisation is key, as are the traditional forms, chords, and scales of the blues. One of the most common forms in blues is a progression called the *12-bar blues,* based on the I, IV, and V chords of the key:

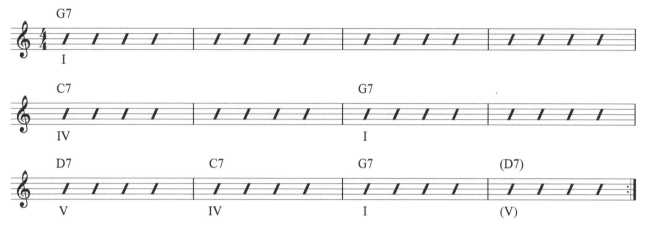

The above progression can be repeated ad infinitum to form a complete song, and other ideas can be added to form intros, bridges, etc. Likewise, it can be shortened (to eight bars, or any other length) or extended depending on style and preference. This progression may also be modified in various ways, still retaining the same basic structure.

Comping

Boogie Patterns

One of the foundations of blues piano is the so-called *boogie pattern*—a left-hand idea that moves from the 5th to the 6th to the ♭7th of each chord, doubling what the bassist would play. A 5th-to-7th boogie pattern not only outlines the root movement of the progression, it adds melodic interest and strongly implies the dominant seventh of each chord.

Here's a basic 12-bar blues in the key of G that uses a boogie pattern. The rhythm is straight eighth notes, but notice the articulation: a staccato feel on the downbeats followed by an accent with tenuto on the offbeats, creating a "short-long" feel. The right hand mimics the 5th-to-♭7th motion of the left, harmonized in thirds.

TRACK 31

Shuffle Feel

Here's another version of the 5th-to-7th style. This example is in a slower, *shuffle* tempo—with a triplet, or 12/8, feel in the left hand. The right hand plays more of a riff/melody with longer note values. The thirds are derived from the triads, with occasional passing tones. This eight-bar example could easily be modified to a full-length 12-bar blues.

TRACK 32

Cut Boogie

Here's another straight eighth-note 12-bar blues. This time, the left hand plays a *cut boogie*, or 5th-to-6th, pattern. The right hand plays sixths derived from the chords, and includes some chromaticism.

TRACK 33

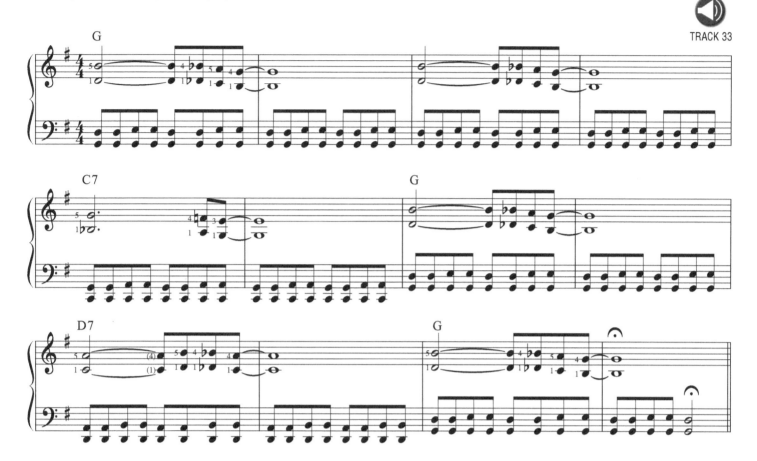

Intro/Turnaround

This example in the key of C sheds some light on "intro" and "turnaround" parts in blues rock (a *turnaround*, you'll recall, leads back to the beginning of a tune, usually via the V chord). The triplet riff that starts this figure is great for a swing or shuffle blues. The A♭7 chord gives you a chromatic approach to the V chord (G7)—the ultimate chord of the turnaround, which sets up the start of the next verse, chorus, etc. (Alternatively, you could approach the V chord with from a half step below—F♯7.)

TRACK 34

Walking Bass

Remember the walking bass? Here's a unique take on that idea called the *flat-tire rhythm*. This type of rhythm dates back to early blues players such as Pinetop Perkins and Professor Longhair, and was later reinterpreted by many modern blues rock keyboardists.

TRACK 35

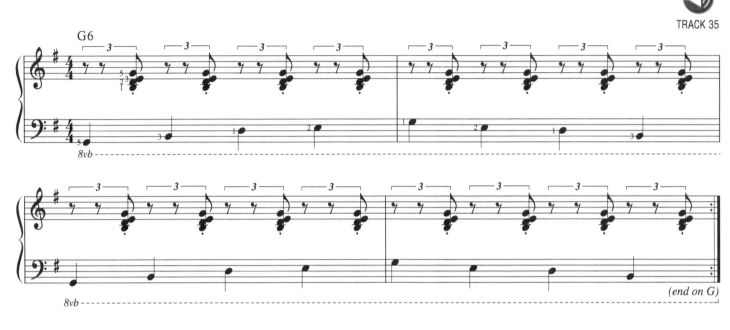

Here's another idea based on the same walking bass line. Incidentally, on a single-chord vamp like this, a walking bass that moves 1–3–5–6 may be just what the doctor ordered.

TRACK 36

Twisting the Progression

Blues rock doesn't have to stick to traditional blues progressions exclusively. This idea is a twist on an 8-bar blues. The turnaround veers off into some unusual territory: Am7–B♭7–F.

TRACK 37

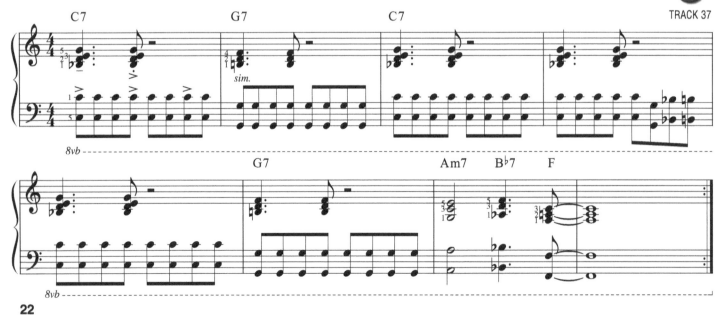

Minor/Dorian Vamps

When played with the right tone, i–IV Dorian vamps can give off a strong blues vibe and make great beds for improvisation. (Remember the minor pentatonic and blues scales?) The first vamp is in G minor; the second, in C minor. Play both of these with a swing feel. Notice the difference in chord voicings.

More Walking Bass

These examples should give you a solid feel for how to approach a walking bass in a blues rock style—and what to play on top of one. Each is a full 12-bar blues; the second slightly jazzier than the first (the turn-around at the end is a standard I–VI–II–V). Practice the left hand separately until you are confident with the parts.

Soloing

Soloing in a blues rock setting is usually done by creating different lines based off of a blues scale. Practice the first set of ideas below in the key of C, as shown, then try them in other keys (see Scales at the end of this book). They may sound confined at first, but soon you will be able to improvise out of the blues scales with increased dexterity, adding your own notes and rhythmic interpretations.

The Blues Scale

Here it is again: the C blues scale. Once you have it under your fingers, try the two phrases shown. Then try the final example, which mixes the blues scale with chord tones, over a I-IV progression. (Check out the rootless voicings in the left hand!)

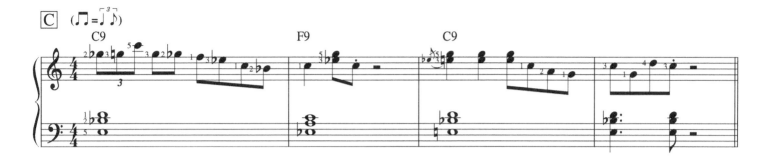

Three Phrases

Keep in mind, a 12-bar blues form consists of three basic phrases (each four bars long). The following 12-bar blues in C takes one of the previous right-hand licks and applies it throughout.

TRACK 41

Double Stops and Grace Notes

Here's another shuffle idea, this one in triplets. The key is F, and the form is blues-based. Half-step movement within the double stops, as well as the use of grace notes, give these licks a "bent-note" sort of sound. Over the B♭ chord, the ♭3rd and 3rd are mixed, and the ♭7th and 5th are targeted.

TRACK 42

Blues-Influenced Minor

There's more than one way to sound bluesy. Here's a minor progression based on a descending chromatic bass (in F). Try the F blues scale over it.

TRACK 43

Chapter 4
SOUTHERN ROCK

À la Marshall Tucker, The Allman Brothers, Lynyrd Skynyrd, The Doobie Brothers, and more...

Southern rock is a great style for the keyboardist—piano and organ play an essential role in any Southern rock rhythm section, and the vocabulary couldn't be more basic or more versatile. Triads, seventh chords, diatonic chord progressions (especially I–IV), thirds and sixths, etc. will go a long way in this genre. Familiarity with these elements will translate to many other styles as well.

Comping

I-IV Progressions

One characteristic of Southern rock is tonic (I) to subdominant (IV) chord motion. This rollicking piano part in the key of F is a great example. There are basically four phrases: The first is based on the tonic, oscillating between I and IV (F to B♭). The next phrase follows the same pattern but from the subdominant (B♭ to E♭), before returning to the tonic. The third phrase stays on B♭, and the last phrase wraps up on F. The V chord (C) is used transitionally and adds a sense of finality to the last phrase.

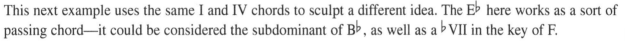

TRACK 44

This next example uses the same I and IV chords to sculpt a different idea. The E♭ here works as a sort of passing chord—it could be considered the subdominant of B♭, as well as a ♭VII in the key of F.

TRACK 45

Here's one more version of I-to-IV chord motion, with an E♭ thrown in. This example is in 3/4 time.

Other Diatonic Motion

Of course, there's a lot more to Southern rock than just I and IV chords. Other diatonic chord motion is common—like the following I–V–vi–IV progression in the key of C. Notice here though, that the basic idea is still moving from I to IV (C to F). Interesting!

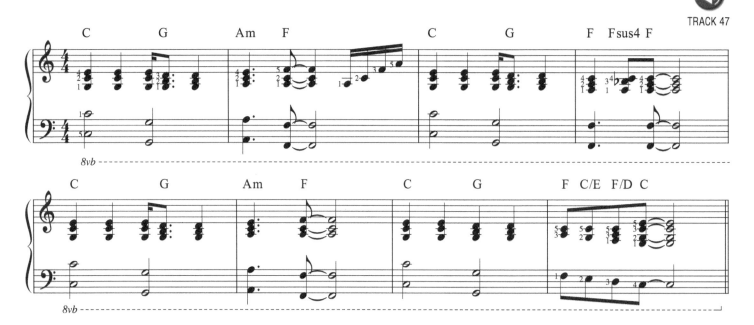

These next two examples are two variations on a IV-V-I progression in the key of C (F–G–C). Of special interest is the pickup measure, which has a bass *walk-up*, first harmonized in thirds, and then in full chords. The 3/4 meter gives the whole thing a "waltz" feel, which makes this great ballad material. Use a piano/organ patch on your keyboard, blending the two tones.

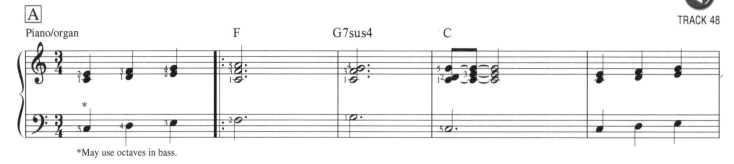

28

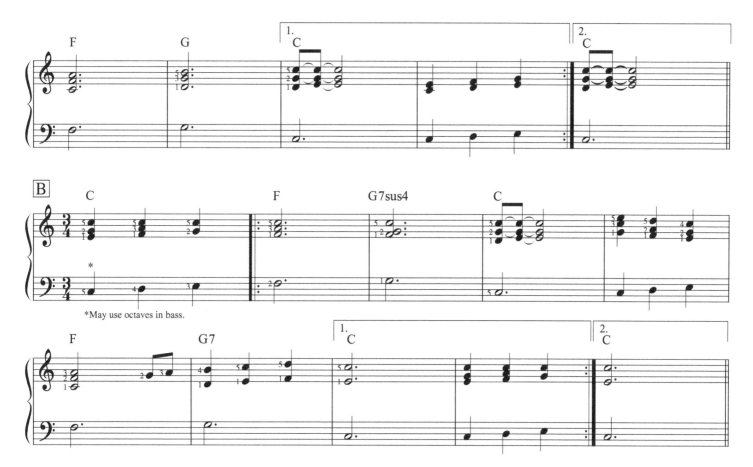

Stride

Stride is a traditional piano style conducive to some Southern rock tunes. (The label "stride" refers to the large intervals played by the left hand.) First try the "jumping" left hand part by itself—start slowly and work towards accuracy. Then move on to both hands. Notice the sixteenth-note anticipation in the right hand. Also notice the emphasis here on dominant seventh chords.

TRACK 49

Here's a nice ending lick based on an F7. The left-hand stride part is slowed down to quarter notes.

TRACK 50

Organ Pad

When in doubt, try an organ "pad." This driving example in 3/4 time would make a great backing to an intro, solo, or ending section. The whole-note chords really allow it to breathe. Play it with a heavy, Hammond organ sound. If you don't have an actual Hammond, try different organ patches on your keyboard or synth.

TRACK 51

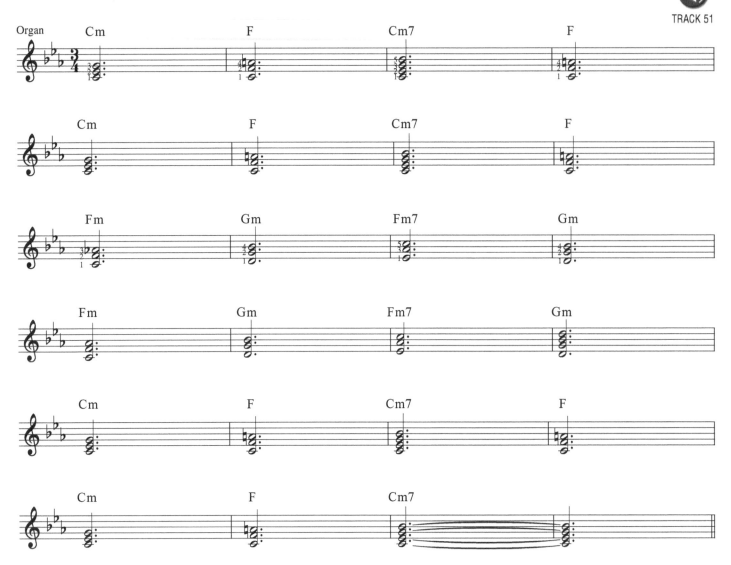

Soloing

Mixing 3rds

Seventh chords are always welcome in Southern rock, and a great sound over them is the mixing of the major and minor third. Here, the chord motion is I–IV–I in the key of F, and the 3rd and ♭3rd (the notes A and A♭) are mixed freely over the tonic. Of course, over the B♭7, you'll want to stick with an A♭, as it's the flat seventh of the chord.

TRACK 52

Sixths

The interval of a sixth is another safe bet in Southern rock. Start with the 3rd and 5th of the underlying harmony (in this case, a C chord), and see where it takes you. Notice how these particular intervals move chromatically in a downward motion—a little bit of a blues influence, for sure.

TRACK 53

Here's an extrapolation of the previous idea, alternating chordal licks with chromatic sixths—this time in the key of F.

TRACK 54

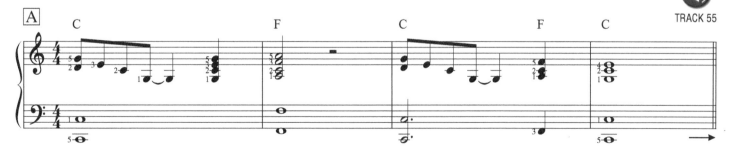

Added Seconds

The second is always a great interval for adding a little color to a chordal idea (you probably noticed it already in some of the previous comping examples). Try it on this I–IV progression in the key of C. Then try the second example, a more inspired take on the idea.

TRACK 55

More Riffs & Licks

Here are some additional right-hand ideas. If you want to add a left-hand part to these, follow the chord symbols, playing simple triads or dominant seventh voicings.

The first phrase uses a chromatic approach to the sixth interval over C7 and F7 chords, followed by diatonic sixths over the G7 chord.

TRACK 56

This one has a bit of everything. Notice the use of the note A over the C chord. This non-chord tone (the 6th) is a common Southern rock flavor.

There's a lot of mixing of the major and minor third going on in this one.

Chapter 5

HARD ROCK

À la the Black Crowes, Van Halen, Journey, Deep Purple, Queen, Led Zeppelin, Boston, REO Speedwagon, Bad Company, and more…

Tougher and more driving than other forms of rock, hard rock attains some of its edge through its harmonic and melodic choices. Hard rock tends to favor simple chords—guitarists, for example, often play simple two-note power chords—but its progressions can be less predictable, often reflecting a mixing of tonalities (e.g., the use of ♭VI and ♭VII chords).

For a typical hard rock vamp or riff, organ is the instrument of choice. Be warned, however, hard rock also has its traditional side, and the occasional piano interlude is always a possibility.

Comping

I–♭VII Progressions

Hard rock vamps often make use of the ♭VII chord. The ♭VII—in the key of G, for example, an F chord—doesn't belong to the major key, but it does belong to the Mixolydian mode as well as the natural minor (e.g., G Mixolydian or G natural minor). Often, the ♭VI chord (e.g., E♭) appears in conjunction with the ♭VII; this is another chord "borrowed" from the natural minor.

The following I–♭VII phrase works well with a pedal point bass line, where the bass stays on the tonic note (G) throughout most of the piece. Sus 4's extend the harmony and give the idea a melodic hook. Notice the ♭VI–♭VII–I cadence at the end of the vamp.

TRACK 57

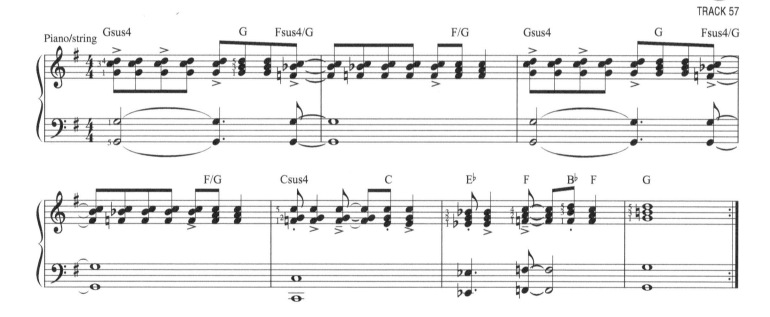

This next piece might seem very different from the previous one on the surface, but its structure is surprisingly similar. The left hand again plays a pedal point (this time, C), while the right—instead of playing sus4 chords and triads—plays hollow-sounding fourths that imply first the minor tonic (Cm) and then the ♭VII (B♭). Then, as the right hand continues to alternate between fourths, the left-hand bass moves down for a ♭VI–♭VII–I cadence.

Notice the use of the bass clef for both hands. This lower register, darker piece is played pianissimo, with a legato feel—try playing the notes as connected as possible.

TRACK 58

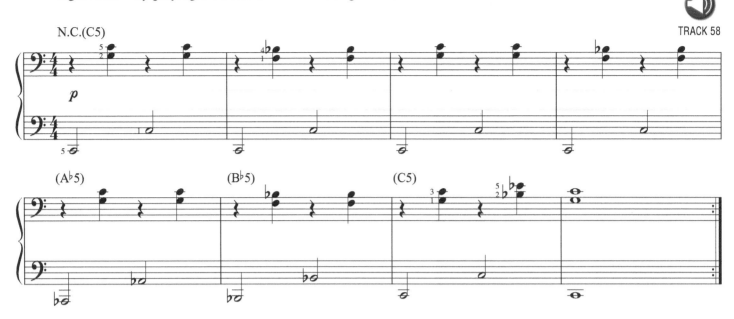

More Pedal Points

Pedal points will work with more than just I–♭VII ideas. In fact, they're great for I–IV progressions (the pedal tone is usually the tonic, which belongs to both chords). This next example is essentially a vamp in C. The first bar acts as a pickup to the main I7–IV–I idea, which later becomes a IVsus4–IV–I idea. Use a bit of overdrive on your keyboard or amp to help simulate the overdriven Hammond B3 tone.

TRACK 59

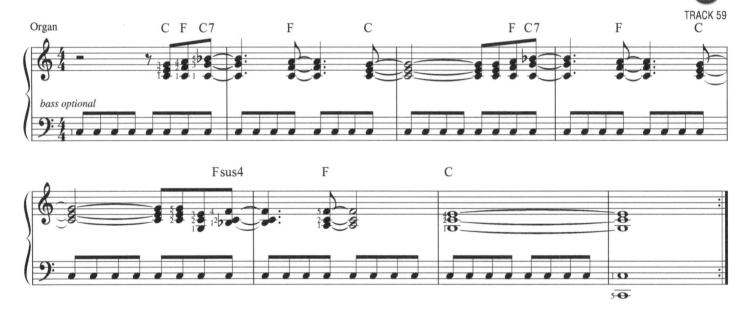

Here's a more rhythmically active pedal point bass. The progression should be familiar by now: it's essentially C–B♭–A♭–C, or I–♭VII–♭VI–I, the reverse of what we've been playing. Each chord is ornamented by its IV chord, for a little "sus4" action. (The exception is A♭—it moves to B♭ to avoid the dissonance of a D♭ chord against the C pedal!)

TRACK 60

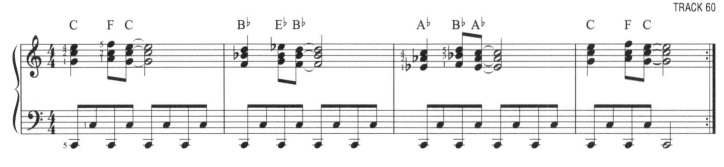

Once again, here's another way of moving from I to IV. Try using an organ tone on your keyboard—but if you do, leave out the optional bass.

Inversions

A lot of keyboard parts in hard rock are for the right hand only—especially when using an organ sound. The following examples play around with using different triad inversions in the right hand, to create parts that are both harmonic and melodic.

This first one is in D minor. It moves between i and ♭VII, then to the familiar ♭VI (in measure 5, the bassist plays a G note, making the B♭ sound like a Gm7).

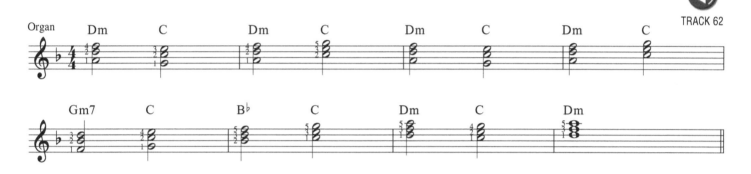

Here's a similar idea, this time in D major. This one has a swing feel and a rhythmically strong groove. Use a distorted or overdriven organ patch on your keyboard.

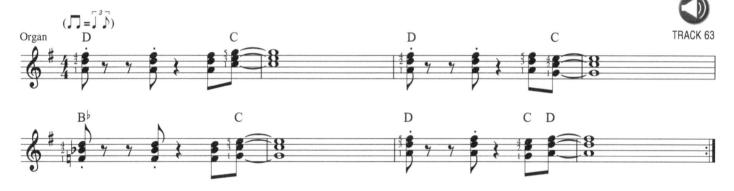

Here's a variation with a D minor sound—actually, the Em chord makes this technically a Dorian groove. (Confused? The relative major key would be C.)

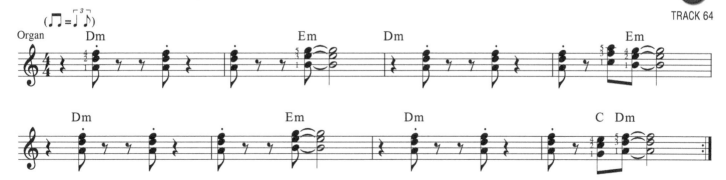

Minor Keys

As mentioned, hard rock is not without its thoughtful, moody moments. For those times, it's great to pull out a minor-key progression like this one in G minor. The right hand uses three- and four-note voicings economically—letting the bass in the left hand define some of the harmonic motion. Back to playing with both hands!

TRACK 65

Soloing

I–♭VII Ideas

This two-handed lick has a vaguely minor-ish sound. The right hand plays a 2nd/5th cluster, while the bass moves from C to B♭ to C. The third measure adds a little variation for fun.

TRACK 66

Here's a ♭VI–♭VII–I progression in D major with a melody on top. Notice the F and C notes in the melody. These are flatted (from D major) to accommodate the B♭ and C chords. Given that the ♭VI and ♭VII are "borrowed" from the parallel minor, you could consider playing in D minor for the first two measures, and in D major for the next two.

TRACK 67

Blues Licks

Blues licks are great for great for "stops" or "breaks" in a hard rock tune. Here are a few related ideas in D blues with a fairly heavy sound.

TRACK 68

The following piece really doesn't know if it's in C minor or C Dorian. In either case, a C blues scale works great for fills and for the iv–v–♭VI–♭VII (Fm–Gm–A♭–B♭) walk-up.

TRACK 69

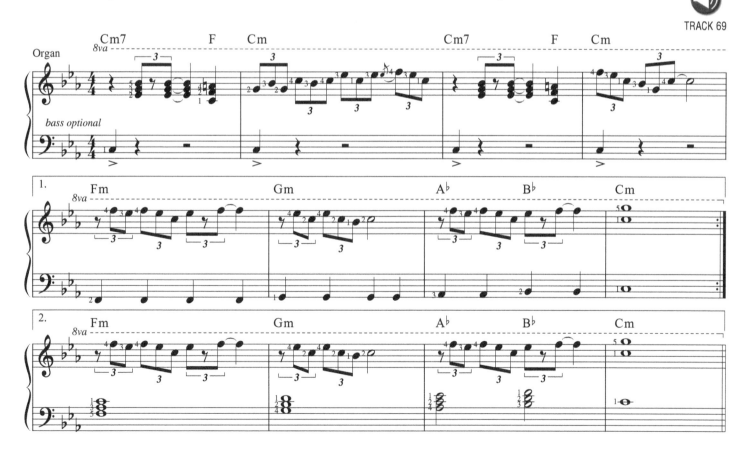

Sixteenth-Note Arpeggios

Sometimes, the line between one type of rock and the next gets a bit blurry. The following ideas could just as well be progressive rock (see the next chapter), but they have their place in hard rock, too. They're all sixteenth-note arpeggios in D minor. You'll see the ♭VII and ♭VI here, among other chords.

TRACK 70

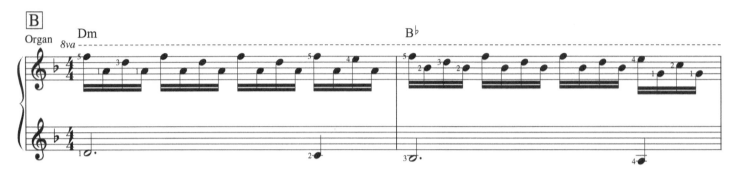

Chapter 6

PROGRESSIVE ROCK

À la Yes, Kansas, Rush, Journey, Toto, Steely Dan, etc.

Progressive rock—or art rock as it's sometimes called—is about expanding boundaries. Musically, progressive rock always retains the basic feel of rock, but it borrows heavily from other styles—like funk, jazz, and classical music. Other hallmarks of the genre include advanced song forms, literate and ambitious lyrics, and instrumental virtuosity.

Comping

The Funk Influence

Don't let all the notes fool you; in this example, the right hand is really just vamping in and around a Gm9 chord—but using triadic voicings, beginning with one based on the third of the chord (B♭). The chord of emphasis is really what looks like a Dm—this is the 2nd, 5th, and 7th of the Gm9 chord. The bass plays the root G throughout. The other chord (what looks like a C) is just a passing chord, giving the line a melodic cohesiveness—as well as that Dorian edge. ("Why Dorian?" you ask. A ♭6th would probably just sound too dissonant!)

The rhythm section here really cooks in full-funk mode, but this type of accompaniment is also typical of bands like Yes or Kansas, and might be played as a verse underneath a vocal part, so its simplicity works well in the right context.

TRACK 71

*Bass plays G root throughout.

Getting Jazzier

This example shows the jazzier side of progressive rock, à la Steely Dan—a minor i–V vamp dressed up with a 7♯9 voicing. The sixteenth-note rhythm makes the groove happen. Notice we're again using triads in the right hand (e.g., B♭) to imply seventh or extended chord qualities.

TRACK 72

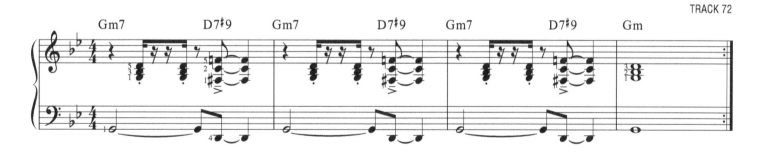

Two-Handed Chords

Here's another example of how bands such as Steely Dan or Toto might phrase a keyboard accompaniment. Using both hands, play these "long-short" eighth-note rhythms in sync with the bass. Make sure you're playing with the correct accidentals in the key signature (B♭ and E♭). This is a ♭VII–i vamp in G minor; your left hand is typically playing the 6th of each chord while the bass guitar is supplying the actual roots.

TRACK 73

*Bass guitar plays roots.

Here's one more two-handed "chord punch" idea. The key is the same, but the chords are even more unusual. They're essentially built in fourths—quartal. Notice the contrary motion between the two hands.

TRACK 74

Dorian Vamps

Here are two takes on the same basic i–ii idea in C Dorian. The first is just a straight pad; the second adds a bit of rhythm. Notice the underlying rhythmic feel and the phrasings here; these distinguish this type of chord idea from similar ideas in the "pseudo-jazz" classic rock genre.

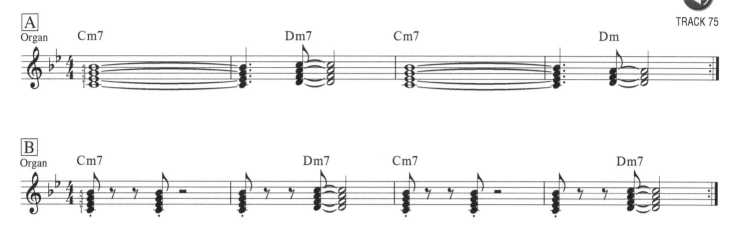

The Classical Influence

This elegant progression in A minor shows the classical side of progressive rock. Notice the top note of each chord—this is the implied melody. Over Am–G–F, the melody moves from the 3rd (C) to the root (A); over Dm–C–B♭, the melody moves from the 4th (D) to the ♭2nd (B♭). It never seems to get to the root when the Am chord is there! Incidentally, the part may sound complex, but notice how each well each i–♭VI–♭VII progression fits under the hand.

TRACK 76

The Bounce

We've seen these ideas before, but never quite like this—a i–IV–i7–IV vamp over a tonic pedal tone. What's unique here is the rhythmic exchange between right and left hands as they trade off on octave A's in a triplet rhythm—a.k.a. the "bounce." Beats 2 and 4 get the most emphasis—creating a rising and falling chordal motion—while the bounce creates an exciting, uneasy minor backdrop. Think of Kansas or Toto for this one.

TRACK 77

Soloing

As mentioned before, progressive rock is about virtuosity. These sixteenth-note ideas will get you started in the right direction.

Pedal Point

If rock has two favorite modes, they are Dorian and Mixolydian. We saw this figure in Dorian earlier; now here it is in Mixolydian: I–IV–I7–IV over a simple tonic pedal in D. (Here's something else to think about: Notice the top note pattern: 5–6–♭7. What is this but an elaborated boogie bass?)

These chords should fit comfortably in the right hand. Nevertheless, at a brisk tempo, this sixteenth-note rhythm can be a workout. The band breaks on beat 1 of the third measure, leaving the keyboard to play by itself; keep your tempo solid through this area of the tune. If you have access to a Hammond or digitial organ, play this figure using a "full stop" setting. If possible, use a "slow speed" on your Leslie.

TRACK 78

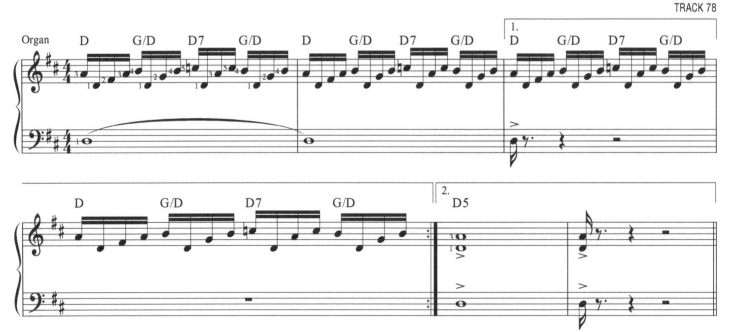

Descending Minor Progression

Here's a statelier number in A minor. This one has some really nice twist and turns. The basic idea is a descent from the i chord to the V chord, resolving to the i. The bass line moves chromatically while the top note of each chord makes a more gradual descent. By the way, do you notice the interrupted sequence here? First Am moves to its V chord (in first inversion), E/G#. Then G moves to its V chord, D/F#. You'd think the same thing might happen with F—but no, we get E7, the V chord of Am, which takes us back home.

Play this with a light, lead organ tone. This tune is in 2/4 time and uses a sixteenth-note triplet rhythm. It should give you a good idea of how to play a solo line in a style similar to bands like Kansas or Yes.

TRACK 79

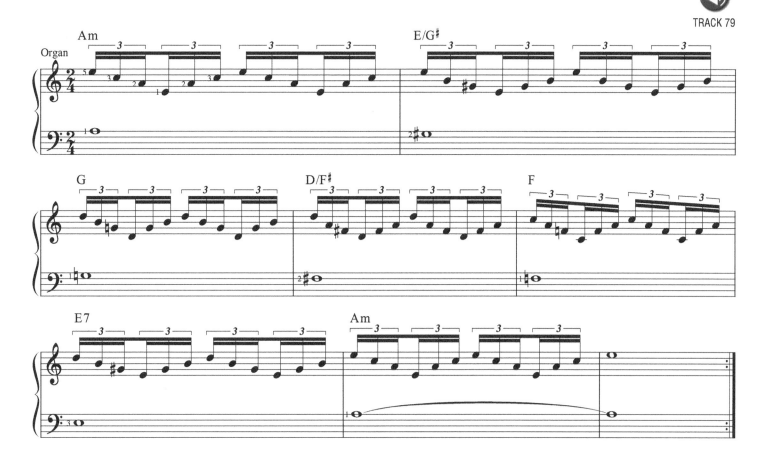

A "Modal" Approach

Here, the right hand plays a sus4 or "modal" idea—a C arpeggio with an added F note—which fits well over the left hand shells. The basic progression is I–IV in the key of C, with a $\flat$VII (B$\flat$) implied at the end.

TRACK 80

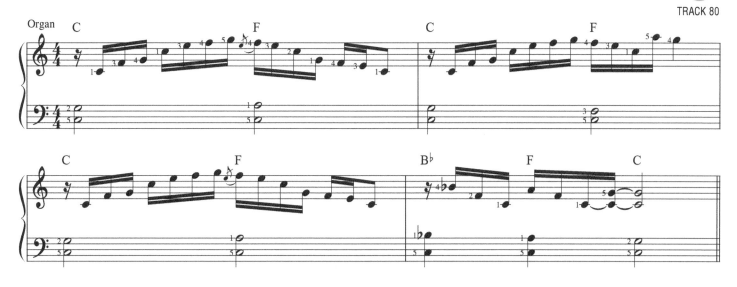

Minor ii-V-i

Here's a slower ballad idea à la Steely Dan. Over this minor ii-V-i turnaround, the right hand plays predominantly chord tones, with a blue note (♭5) thrown in.

TRACK 81

Chapter 7

ALTERNATIVE ROCK

À la Dave Matthews Band, David Gray, Pearl Jam, U2, the Red Hot Chili Peppers, Train, Lenny Kravitz, and more…

Alternative rock generally leans on guitar-heavy production. Keyboard parts in this style might be layered lightly in the mix and used as "filler" or coloring. This creates the opportunity to add tension to a song or broaden the sound of the guitar. Some of the following tracks use a very simplistic pad approach; others get into more percussive-type grooves. String, organ and piano tones are useful, or try using any keyboard patch you desire.

Comping

Dissonant Layering

Pads are a great way of filling out a sound while still leaving a lot of space for other instruments in the band—like guitar and drums. Using long note values (mostly whole and half notes) and a sustaining "piano/strings" sound, these next two parts allow the groove to "breathe," while also adding some unusual tensions—in particular, the 9th.

This first tune is basically a vi–IV–ii–V progression in C major but with the 9th added and even doubled in just about every chord (the first bar, for example, has an Am chord with a B natural on the top of both the right and left hands). Wide intervals in both hands—notice the simple right-hand shells—and frequently omitted 3rds add up to a hollow, almost restless sound.

TRACK 82

Here's a similar idea, using a I-IV progression in G with a ♭VI–♭VII–I cadence. This time, the right hand is playing slightly fuller voicings and moving more economically, but the 9th again plays a role. This type of "open" part sounds great with an active sixteenth-note hi-hat.

TRACK 83

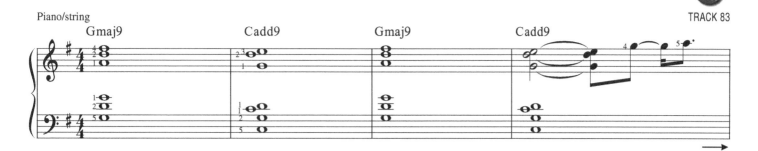

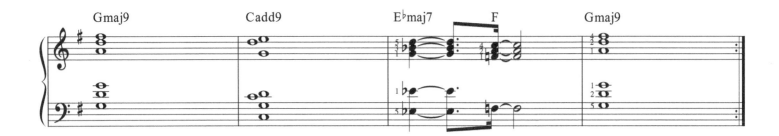

The All-Purpose Vamp

A rhythmically active vamp is always a great thing to have at the ready. This very conventional progression (I–V–vi–IV in the key of C) could just as well be Motown as alternative rock—the feel is very laid back and the organ tone is smooth. How about those major sevenths and ninths at the end?

TRACK 84

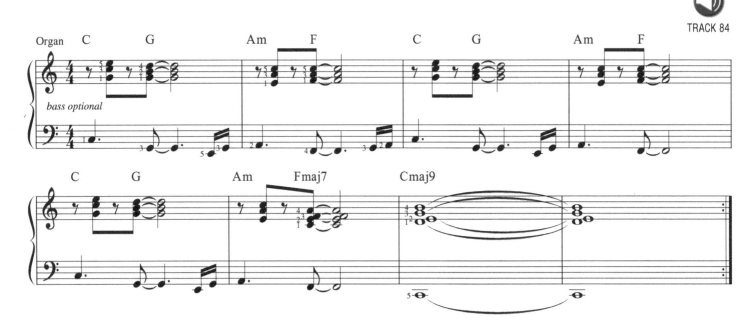

I-IV Inversions

Here's an interesting line sculpted out of a I–IV (C-F) chord move in the right hand. The key is C, but the F chord gets a lot of emphasis due to the rhythmic anticipation. Variations add life to this line; notice in measure 4, C gets replaced by B♭ (the ♭VII), marking the end of a four-bar phrase. In the next phrase, the inversions start moving around, creating melodic interest.

TRACK 85

Low Piano

Here's a fairly simple accompaniment in the key of C using sparse voicings and a descending bass that leads from I to IV to ♭VII to IV. The real distinguishing feature here is the low register (notice both hands are in bass clef), which has a great sound on piano and leaves plenty of room for guitar and a vocal on top. Be sure to observe the 3/4 meter!

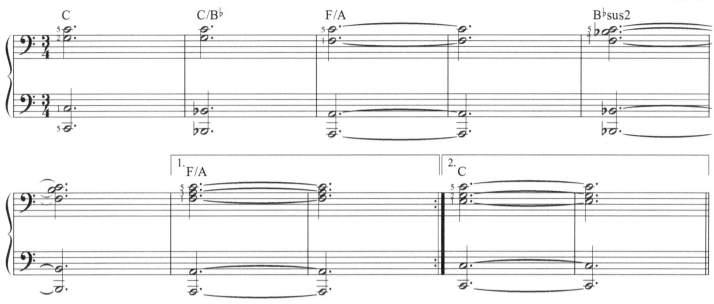

Percussive Organ

For a funkier sound, a percussive right-hand organ part like this one is a must. The progression is basically a Dorian i7–IV7 vamp (in Gm) leading to a ♭VI–♭VII–i cadence. Check out the voicings: mostly dyads using very economical hand motion, played with sparse rhythm. Let the bassist supply the root notes, while the guitarist scratches chords in sixteenth-note rhythms.

TRACK 87

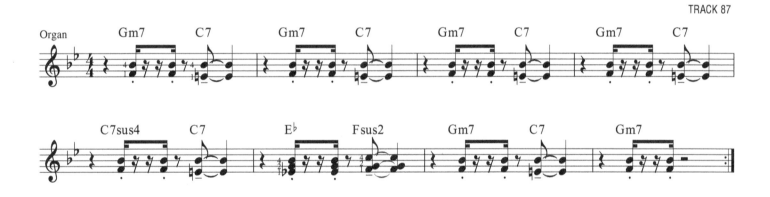

Soloing

Alternative rock usually favors a strong melodic "hook" over an extended, improvised solo; nevertheless, good licks always have a place in any style.

Fills

At times, it's necessary to use a chord accompaniment along with your solo line—both in the same hand. Practice the following right-hand chord stabs first (another funk-inspired Dorian i–IV vamp in Gm—the "hook" of the tune). Then try adding the solo fills, which are based on the minor pentatonic in the same basic hand position.

TRACK 88

Three-Note Patterns

A great way to get started on a solo idea is to use a three-note pattern in a meter based in four. Here's a sixteenth-note idea born from that concept. It starts over a Gm chord, using an A–B♭–G pattern in the right hand. (Notice the tension of the 9th!) The pattern is modified where necessary to follow the descending bass, but in some cases, it remains static, letting the bass alone redefine the harmony. The top note becomes the melody, which is distinctly syncopated thanks to the rhythmic displacement of "three" against "four."

Harmonically, the seconds (e.g., A–B♭) really create a lot of dissonance, but notice how things "open up" briefly in the fourth bar—the C chord feels like an oasis in the desert!

TRACK 89

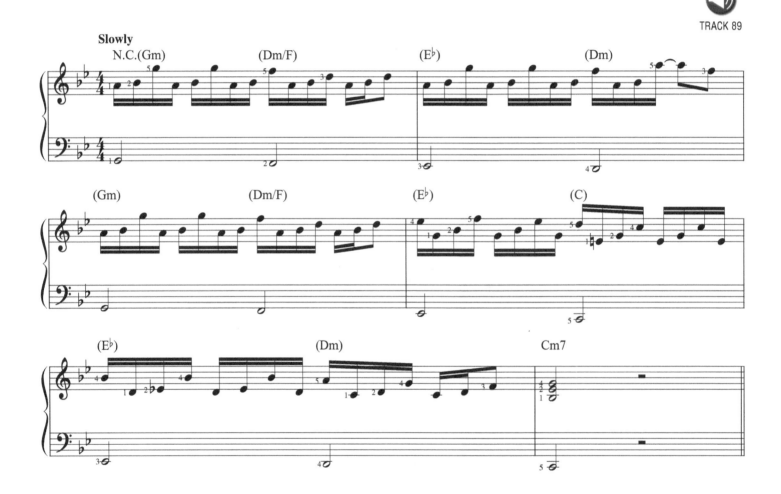

Chapter 8

HEAVY METAL

À la Metallica, Megadeth, Pantera, Stone Temple Pilots, Smashing Pumpkins, Queensryche, Judas Priest, Ozzy Osbourne, and more…

Heavy metal may not seem the most keyboard-friendly of rock styles, but that can make it all the more interesting as a player. Dissonant pads, unusual progressions, sixteenth-note punches, minor riffs… these are some of the keyboardist's tools in the genre of metal. When you can hold your own in this style, you can consider yourself a well-rounded rock keyboardist.

Comping

Right-Hand Clusters (Texture)

The following tune has a minor/Dorian feel; the bass jams modally against an implied D pedal—even grabbing a ♭5th (A♭) from the D blues scale—while the guitarist riffs in a similar vein. The keyboardist's job is to lay down a pad on top. A string patch will add a nice texture to the phrase; then all you have to do is hold down long, whole note rhythms. I chose ambiguous chord clusters favoring 2nds and 4ths—essentially, these are just various suspensions of a Dm7 chord, which finally resolve on a Dm9 (a.k.a., Fm7/D).

The bass line is optional here, but playing it will give you a better understanding of the "groove" of the tune. If you like, try saving it until the repeat; notice how the tune becomes even heavier.

TRACK 90

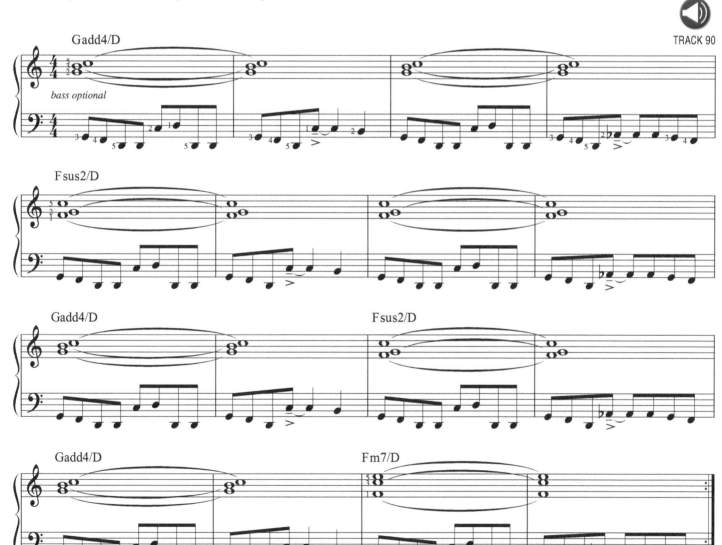

Dissonant Suspension

Here's another pad, but this one is more prominent. It's really driving the tune (a distorted organ tone helps!). The band joins together on this groove with heavy accents on beat 1 of every other measure. On the repeat, the snare kicks in on beats 2 and 4.

The main idea here is really just a suspended 4th resolving to a major chord, but the 4th (or 11th) in this case is sharped, for a lot of extra bite. You can think of this note (A#) as belonging to the key of B major, so you're playing an E idea but in the key of B. (For those keeping track of modes, that would be E Lydian.)

TRACK 91

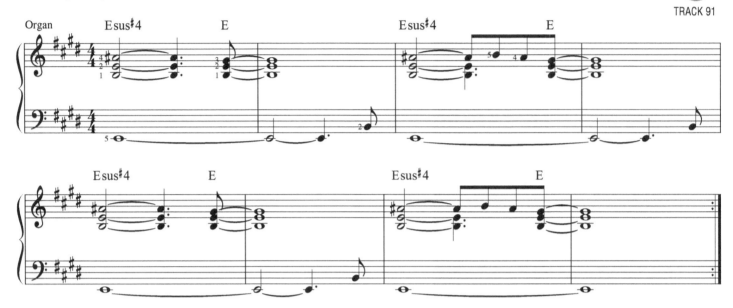

Two-Chord Motives

These next two pieces are more developed. Both employ two-handed chord voicings with added dissonances. The first is in E minor, but starts out with the same E#11-to-E move we saw in the previous example. Nevertheless, the chord progression is rooted in minor.

Notice the first two bars: E to C. Each is its own idea, moving from tension to resolution, but together, they also form a single, descending two-bar melodic idea. In measure 9, the progression moves to new harmonic territory (Am7–Em7–Am7–G), and the melodic direction changes as well, moving up instead of just down.

TRACK 92

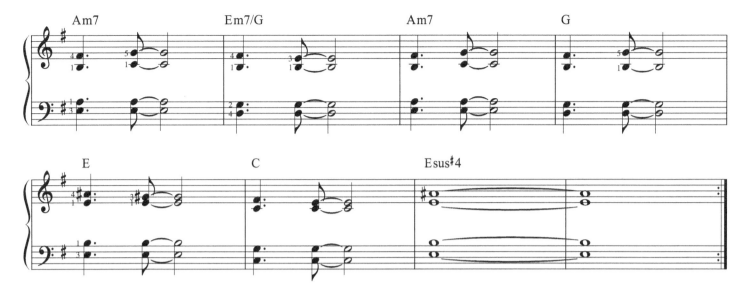

This piece is more clearly in E minor, and uses much the same harmonic movement. The underlying idea is also similar: using tension and resolution over each chord to create a recognizable motive. In this case, a D–F# dyad resolves either up or down to the chord of choice.

The bass line and drum pattern create a "Megadeth" or "Pantera" –style metal rhythm, which allows space for the keyboard part to come through.

TRACK 93

Sixteenth-Note "Punches"

These next two pieces are in D minor and focus on fast, sixteenth-note "punches"—sometimes syncopated—a feel reminiscent of heavy-metal bands such as Metallica.

TRACK 94

Lock in with the "Led Zeppelin"-style octave bass groove on this one. Notice the diatonic chord movement Gm7–F/A–B♭–C–Dm. The A bass note under the F chord is played by the bassist.

TRACK 95

String Pad

This piece uses the same diatonic chord progression as the previous two examples, but played in long, whole- and half-note rhythms, using a string patch on your keyboard. Keyboards are typically used for "layering" in heavy metal styles. This track shows how you can take the same part and make it "blend in" with the band, without being a focal point.

TRACK 96

Soloing

Minor Riffing

Here are some ideas in D minor—well, actually D Dorian. This first vamp shows you the melodic foundation. After getting the feel of it, try using fifths in the left hand to outline the same progression and "riffing" in the right hand. You can use chord tones, notes from the D minor pentatonic or Dorian scales, or even notes from relative major scale, C.

TRACK 97

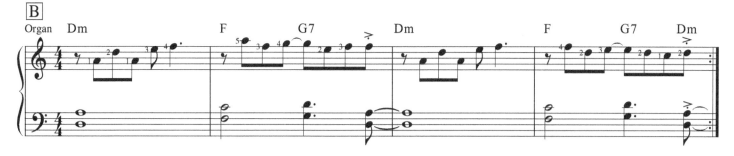

Sixteenth-Note Licks

Here's another minor progression: a i–♭VII vamp in C minor. This first track shows you the accompaniment in the right hand, plus the bass line in the left. Notice how the rhythm pushes with the bass at the end of each bar, with a sixteenth note.

TRACK 98

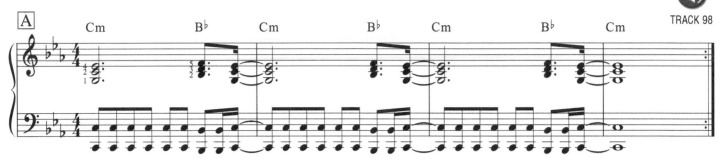

Now switch the triads to your left hand, while playing simple, sixteenth-note licks in the right. The melodic idea here is basically a decoration of the chord progression; all the activity surrounds the chord changes. The key melody notes are E♭ and C.

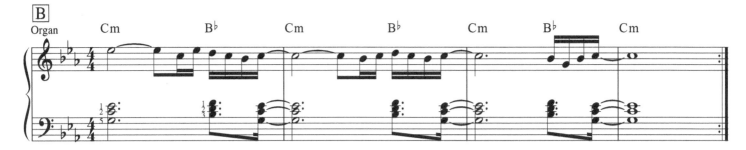

Diatonic Sixths

Here's one last progression in C minor. Play the left hand first, in octaves and fifths. Then try the solo line that follows, built primarily from sixths in a downward motion. Notice the use of arpeggios over the Fm, A♭, and B♭ chords, which fill out the piece and provide some contrast.

With its heavy "theatrical" vibe, this would make a great intro solo—something Black Sabbath or Iron Maiden might have used to open their concerts!

TRACK 99

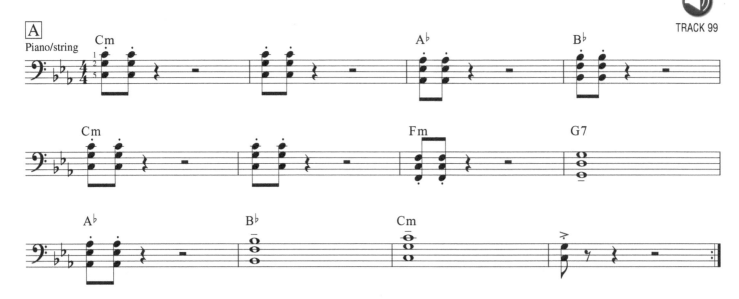

SCALES

The following scales—minor pentatonic and blues—are very common in rock soloing. Practice them in as many keys as you find useful. Fingerings are included for both the right and left hands.

Minor Pentatonic

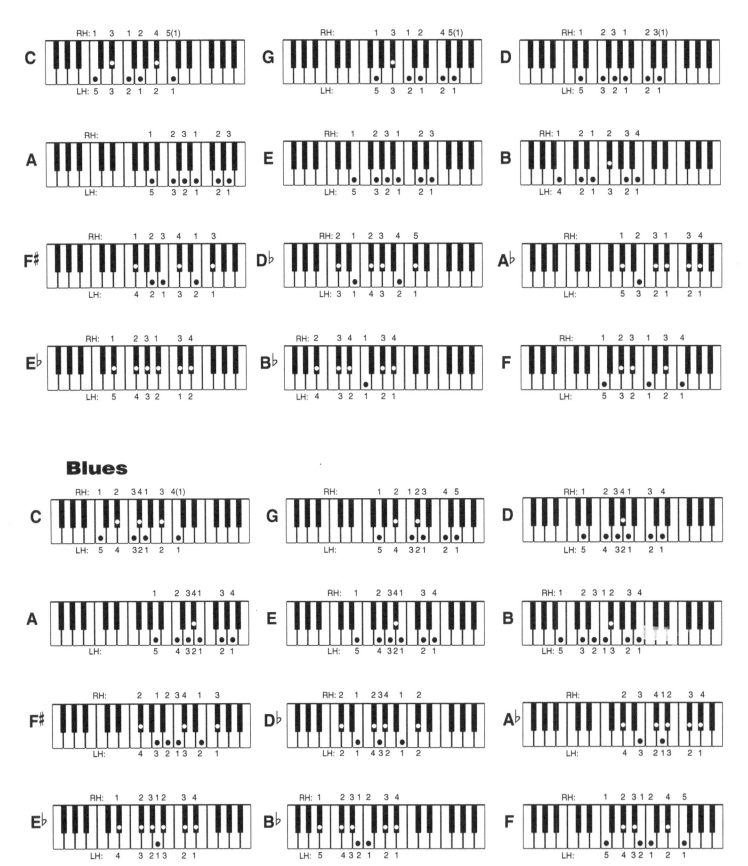

Blues